3/06

DATE DUE

L
3

THE HISTORY OF THE **DENVER BRONCOS**

THE HISTORY OF THE
DENVER

Published by Creative Education
123 South Broad Street
Mankato, Minnesota 56001
Creative Education is an imprint of The Creative Company.

DESIGN AND PRODUCTION BY **EVANSDAY DESIGN**

3-24-06

LIBRARY OF CONGRESS CATALOGING-IN-PUBLICATION DATA

Schmalzbauer, Adam.
The history of the Denver Broncos / by Adam Schmalzbauer.
p. cm. — (NFL today)
Summary: Traces the history of the team from its beginnings through 2003.
ISBN 1-58341-295-6
1. Denver Broncos (Football team)—History—Juvenile literature. [1. Denver
Broncos (Football team)—History. 2. Football—History.] I. Title. II. Series.

GV956.D4S35 2004
796.332'64'0978883—dc22   2003062565

First edition

9 8 7 6 5 4 3 2 1

COVER PHOTO: defensive tackle Trevor Pryce

PHOTOGRAPHS BY
AP/Wide World Photos, Corbis (Bettmann, Steve Boyle/NewSport, UPI/Corbis-Bettmann, Rick Wilking/Reuters),
Getty Images, SportsChrome USA

LOCATED HIGH IN COLORADO'S ROCKY MOUNTAINS, DENVER IS ONE OF AMERICA'S MOST BEAUTIFUL CITIES. FOUNDED AS A TINY CATTLE TOWN, DENVER'S POPULARITY AND POPULATION EXPLODED IN THE 1870S WHEN GOLD AND SILVER DEPOSITS WERE FOUND NEARBY. BY THE 1950S, DENVER WAS A TRULY RICH CITY. IN ADDITION TO ITS BOOMING BUSINESSES, THE "MILE HIGH CITY" BOASTED STUNNING SCENERY, CLEAN AIR, AND NUMEROUS SKI RESORTS. ONE THING THAT WAS MISSING, HOWEVER, WAS A PROFESSIONAL FOOTBALL TEAM.

THAT CHANGED IN 1959, WHEN DENVER BUSINESS-MAN BOB HOWSAM PURCHASED A FRANCHISE IN THE NEWLY FORMED AMERICAN FOOTBALL LEAGUE (AFL). IN AN ATTEMPT TO GENERATE INTEREST IN THE NEW CLUB, HOWSAM ANNOUNCED A PUBLIC "NAME-THE-TEAM" CONTEST IN 1960. THE WINNING SUGGESTION WAS BRONCOS (A REFERENCE TO THE BUCKING HORSES IN THE RODEOS COMMON IN COLORADO), AND THE DENVER BRONCOS HAVE BEEN RUNNING WILD EVER SINCE.

[Running back Jon Keyworth]

AN UGLY BEGINNING >

IN 1960, THE Broncos made history by defeating the Boston Patriots 13–10 in the very first AFL game. After that, though, Denver struggled. Fans saw some great performances by ball-hawking safety Austin "Goose" Gonsoulin (who intercepted four passes in one game), veteran quarterback Frank Tripucka, and sure-handed end Lionel Taylor, but the Broncos ended the season with an AFL-worst 4–9–1 record.

To make matters worse, the Broncos had the ugliest uniforms in the league. The team's general manager had tried to save money by buying used college uniforms. The Broncos' brown jerseys and yellow pants were bad enough, but the worst part was vertically striped stockings so hideous that the players offered to buy their own.

After Denver went 3–11 in its second season, the team hired a new coach named Jack Faulkner. In an effort to light a fire under his young team, Coach Faulkner announced the "Great Sock Barbecue," at which Denver fans were invited to watch the Broncos' hated old socks go up in flames on a giant bonfire at the team's practice field. Inspired by the sock barbecue, the new orange-and-blue Broncos leaped out to a 7–2 start in 1962. Even though the team stumbled late in the season, fan attendance at home games doubled, and Faulkner was named the AFL Coach of the Year.

Unfortunately, no other Broncos season was that successful during the rest of the 1960s. The team was led by five different coaches during the decade, but none could guide the Broncos to a winning record. Although Denver featured such brilliant players as running back Cookie Gilchrist and receiver Al Denson during those years, it finished its opening decade with a collective 39–97–4 record—the worst of any of the eight original AFL teams.

A LITTLE IMPROVEMENT>

REMARKABLY, DESPITE THEIR losing ways, the Broncos' popularity continued to climb. Starting in 1970 and continuing for three decades, every game at Denver's Mile High Stadium would be sold out. One of the reasons for this amazing support would be Denver's ability to attract exciting stars such as running back Floyd Little.

In 1967, the Broncos paid the then-huge sum of $130,000 for Little, who had been a three-time All-American at Syracuse University. When he gained only 381 rushing yards his rookie year, disappointed fans called him the "$130,000 Lemon." In 1968, though, jeers turned to cheers as Little—running behind linemen Larry Kaminski, Bob Young, and Tom Beer—began to tear through opposing defenses. "I remember one play in

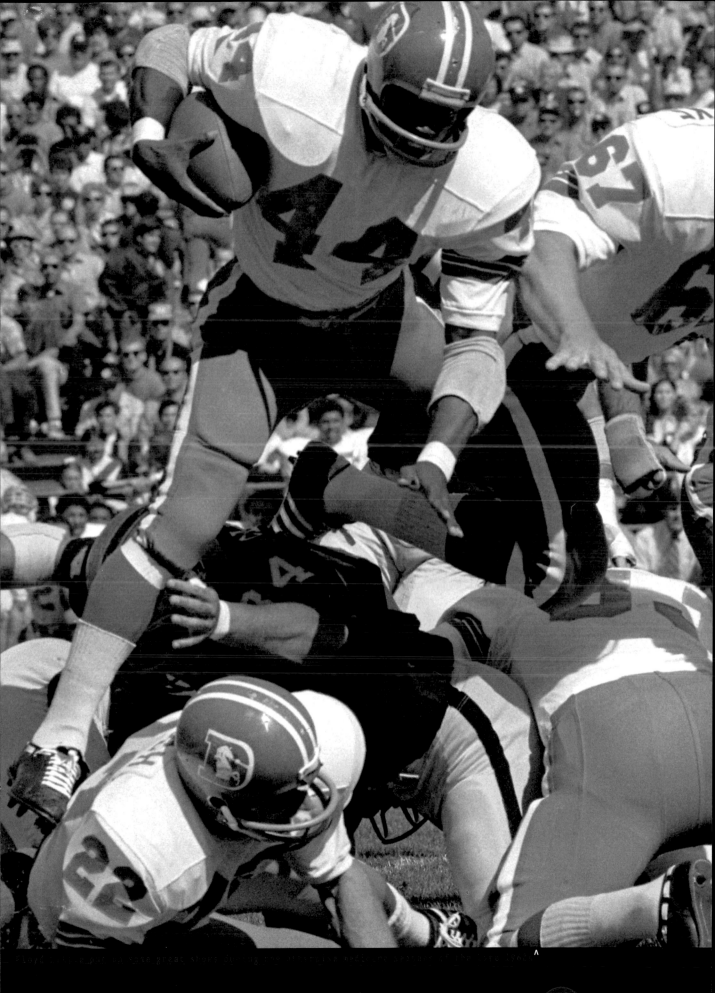

one game late in that 1968 season," Little later re-
called. "It wasn't the length of the run, which was
short, or the game, which was just another game,
but it was the execution of the play. It was per-
fect.... All of a sudden, all the pieces of our jigsaw
puzzle were falling into place."

In 1969, the Broncos kept opposing teams puz-
zled as Little set an AFL record by rushing for 166
yards in a single game. Two years later, Little became Denver's first 1,000-yard rusher. During a
nine-year career in Denver, Little would set team
records with 54 career touchdowns and 6,323 rushing yards, helping the Broncos slowly inch up the
National Football League (NFL) standings (the AFL
had merged with the NFL in 1970). When the player
known as "the Franchise" retired in 1975, the team
retired his number 44 jersey with him.

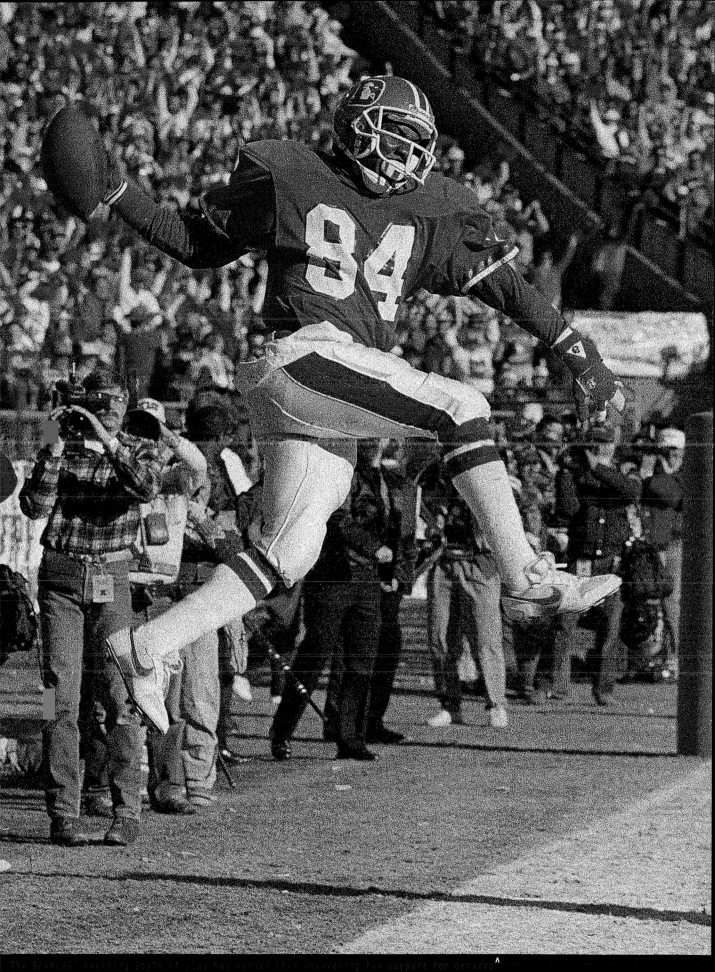

THE HIRING OF DENVER'S eighth head coach, Robert "Red" Miller, in 1977 signaled the start of a new era. That era was dubbed "Broncomania" due to the wild enthusiasm that filled Mile High Stadium at each Broncos home game. Coach Miller helped trigger that excitement before the 1977 season by announcing, "The Broncos will make Denver proud. We're not scared of anyone. We can beat any team."

Miller's players backed up his words, winning the franchise's first American Football Conference (AFC) Western Division title with a 12–2 record. Led by veteran quarterback Craig Morton, Denver's offense was anything but explosive. But with a defense featuring huge linemen Rubin Carter and Lyle Alzado and fearless linebackers Randy Gradishar and Tom Jackson, Denver didn't need to

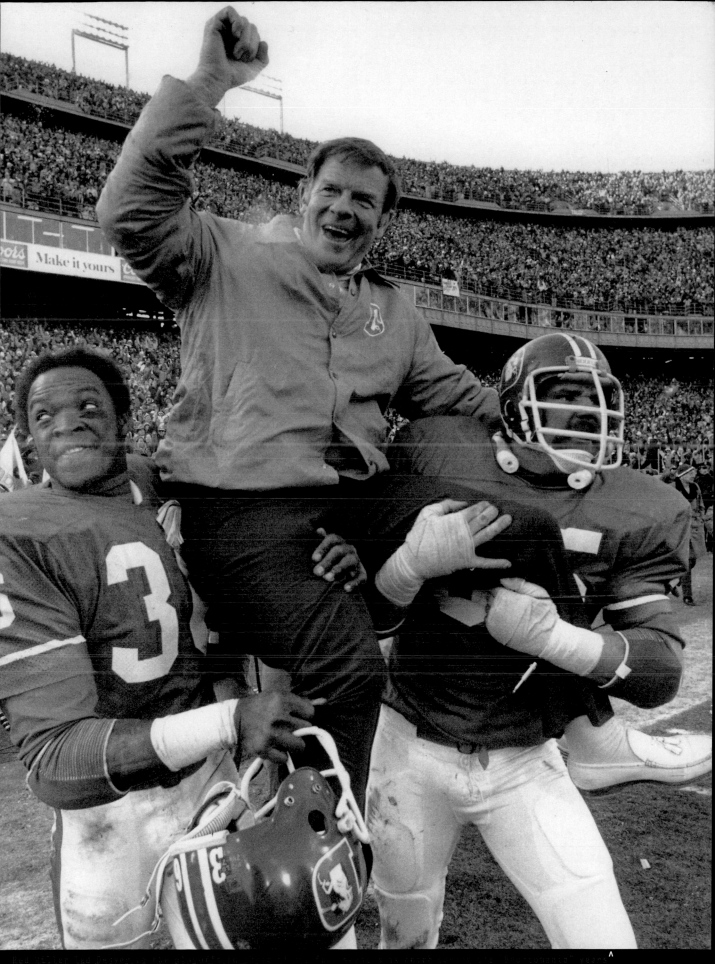

score many points to win. Nicknamed the "Orange Crush" on account of its orange home jerseys and physical style of play, the Denver defense was one of the NFL's most dominant.

When the defending Super Bowl champion Oakland Raiders arrived at Mile High Stadium for the 1977 AFC championship game, all they could see was orange. Denver fans went wild as the Orange Crush held Oakland to a first-half field goal, and the Broncos won 20–17 to advance to the Super Bowl. Unfortunately, the Broncos fell just short of a world championship, losing 27–10 to the veteran Dallas Cowboys in the big game.

Denver powered its way to the playoffs again in 1978 and 1979, posting a 10–6 record each year. Those seasons cemented the Broncos' legacy as one of the NFL's finest teams of the late '70s, even though a Super Bowl victory remained just out of reach.

ELWAY RIDES INTO TOWN>

AFTER DENVER FADED to 8–8 in 1980, Coach Miller was replaced by Dan Reeves. A man with extensive Super Bowl experience, Reeves had played or coached in five Super Bowls with the Dallas Cowboys. When Reeves led the Broncos to an improved 10–6 mark his first year, Denver fans began dreaming of Super Bowl glory once again. Still, many Broncos greats of the '70s had gotten old or moved on, and Denver lacked a true star.

That changed in 1983. That year's NFL Draft produced a number of exceptional quarterbacks, but the Broncos got the one every team wanted: Stanford University standout John Elway. A three-time All-American with a cannon for an arm, Elway became the first pick in the draft when the Baltimore Colts selected him. Elway, feeling the Colts lacked championship potential, announced

Karl Mecklenburg was a defensive force throughout the late '80s, posting 79 career sacks.

that he planned to play baseball instead for the New York Yankees, who had also drafted the multitalented young athlete. Elway had no such plans, but the trick worked as Baltimore traded his rights to Denver.

After Denver made him the NFL's highest-paid rookie, Elway proved his worth by coolly leading the Broncos to the playoffs in 1983. Then, in 1984, the young quarterback guided Denver to the AFC West title with a 13–3 mark. Whether he was launching a deep pass, firing up his teammates, or scrambling for a big gain, Elway expected a lot from himself. "My goal is to beat [Hall of Fame Pittsburgh Steelers quarterback] Terry Bradshaw," Elway said. "He won the Super Bowl four times. I want to win five."

The Broncos made quick exits from the playoffs in 1983 and 1984. Although the team missed the playoffs in 1985, Elway put on a great show, throwing for 3,891 yards and 22 touchdowns, with many of those passes going to receiver Vance Johnson. That was just the start of one of the most remarkable careers in NFL history. In all, the quarterback in the number 7 jersey would spend 16 seasons in the Mile High City, passing for more than 3,000 yards in 12 of them.

Perennial kicker Rich Karlis helped propel the Broncos to the Super Bowl in the 1980s.

In the late 1980s, new defensive stars emerged to help lead the Broncos up the standings. These included linebacker Karl Mecklenburg and safety Dennis Smith. Yet it was Elway who remained the driving force behind the Broncos. As he led the team into the playoffs in 1986, 1987, and 1989, he became known as the "Comeback Kid" due to his knack for rallying the Broncos on game-winning drives late in the fourth quarter.

One such drive took place in the AFC championship game after the 1986 season. Trailing the Cleveland Browns 20–13 with just minutes left, the Broncos got the ball on their own two-yard line. Facing a tough Browns defense, a rowdy Cleveland crowd, and a stiff wind, Elway completed one pressure-packed pass after another to drive Denver the length of the field for the tying touchdown. Barefooted Broncos kicker Rich Karlis then booted a field goal for a 23–20 overtime victory, earning Denver a berth in the Super Bowl against the New York Giants. Unfortunately for Denver fans, the Giants were loaded that year and crushed the Broncos 39–20.

Vance Johnson was Elway's top target in the late '80s ^

THE BRONCOS REBOUNDED from that loss by marching right back to the Super Bowl in 1987 and 1989. Denver fans were again left brokenhearted by the outcomes, though. After the Broncos were crushed by the Washington Redskins and San Francisco 49ers, respectively, some critics wondered if Denver would ever win a Super Bowl. But even as the team put together some mediocre seasons in the early 1990s, Elway and new stars such as tight end Shannon Sharpe and hard-hitting safety Steve Atwater gave fans hope.

In 1995, the Broncos made two key moves that would finally take them to the top. First, they hired Mike Shanahan—the offensive coordinator for the 49ers team that had beaten the Broncos in the 1989 Super Bowl—as the franchise's 11th head coach. Then, in the 1995 NFL Draft, the Broncos found a hidden gem. With the 196th pick, they selected University of Georgia running back Terrell Davis. Called "T.D." by his teammates, Davis quickly gave the Broncos a deadly rushing attack.

In 1996, as linemen Gary Zimmerman and Brian Habib paved the way, Davis charged for 1,538 yards. Behind this heroic effort, the Broncos went 13–3 and won their division before losing to the Jacksonville Jaguars in a playoff upset. Denver dug deeper in 1997 as Davis exploded for 1,750 yards on the season and then powered the Broncos all the way to their fifth Super Bowl. This time Denver faced the defending Super Bowl champion Green Bay Packers.

With the game tied 24–24 in the fourth quarter, Elway became the Comeback Kid once more, marching Denver down the field. Then, with less than two minutes remaining, Davis plunged into the end zone to finally give the Broncos their first world championship. "I'm so proud and happy that

Tackle Trevor Pryce was a quarterback's nightmare ^

Jake Plummer led the 2005 Broncos to the playoffs ^

we could win this for Denver fans and for John," said Davis. "John Elway has meant everything to this franchise, and it's so great to see him finally get what he deserves."

Denver fans found more reasons for celebration the next season. After Davis became the fourth running back in NFL history to rush for 2,000 yards in a season, the Broncos galloped back to the Super Bowl. In what turned out to be Elway's farewell performance, the Hall of Fame quarterback passed for 336 yards in a 34–19 victory over the Atlanta Falcons. After the game, Elway announced his retirement, ending his brilliant career while on top of the football world.

After Elway rode off into the sunset, Davis, defensive tackle Trevor Pryce, and receiver Rod Smith helped keep the Broncos among the AFC's best. In 2000, the team opened the new millennium in fine style by going 11–5. Sadly, Davis would play only one more season before retiring at the age of 29 because of recurring knee problems.

By 2003, Denver had a new offensive leader: former Arizona Cardinals quarterback Jake "the Snake" Plummer, whose confidence, quick feet, and knack for orchestrating comeback victories reminded many fans of Elway. In 2004, the team got a new defensive leader as well by trading young running back Clinton Portis—who had rushed for more than 1,500 yards in both 2002 and 2003—to the Washington Redskins for super-quick cornerback Champ Bailey. With Coach Shanahan guiding these players and linebackers Al Wilson and John Mobley, optimism in Denver remained mile-high.

Although the Broncos left Mile High Stadium for the new INVESCO Field at Mile High in 2001, the Denver faithful continue to pack the bleachers for each and every game. From the Broncomania years to the back-to-back Super Bowl victories of the late '90s, the Broncos have given their loyal fans quite a ride. As a new generation of heroes in orange and blue now get in the saddle, that ride is sure to continue for years to come.

INDEX>